You **Tutorial**

Sewing

THIS IS A CARLTON BOOK

Published in 2015 by Carlton Books Limited
20 Mortimer Street
London W1T 3JT

10 9 8 7 6 5 4 3 2 1

Text and Design © Carlton Books Ltd 2015

A CIP catalogue record for this book is available from the British Library.

ISBN 978 1 78097 511 5

Text by Tessa Evelegh
Senior Executive Editor: Lisa Dyer
Managing Art Director: Lucy Coley
Picture Researcher: Emma Copestake
Production Manager: Janette Burgin
Designer: Emma Wicks
Cover design by Lisa Layton

Printed in Dubai

You Tutorial

Sewing

▶ Your guide to the best instructional YouTube videos

CARLTON BOOKS

Contents

Introduction   6

Tools of the Trade   8

Choosing and Using Patterns   18

Laying Out and Transferring the Markings   32

Stitchery Know-How   41

Basic Techniques   53

Fastenings and Zips   83

Finishing   96

Jeans Genius   102

A Few Fun Projects   108

Credits   128

INTRODUCTION

How to use this book

Whether you want to re-model retro finds, start sewing from scratch or brush up on long-lost skills, here are the 100 very best YouTube videos to get you going. You'll find all the basic techniques clearly demonstrated, from threading a needle to stitching a separating zip and setting in a sleeve. At the end of the book, there is a delectable "menu" of the most innovative DIY sewing projects on YouTube, both for beginners and for those with plenty of sewing savvy. Each video has been chosen for the accuracy of the technique, its clarity and its presentation. We make no apology for featuring some vloggers several times. We trawled the internet for many hours and only after we looked at everything we could find did we come back to them. That's because they really are the best, delivering the technical detail that you can trust. OK, so some might not be the most visually exciting … but that's usually down to the subject matter.

In our YouTube trawls, we've found and met some wonderful people. Some may not (yet) have many views because they have only just started their channel, but if their videos are technically correct, clear and gorgeous to look at, they win a place in this book. Even all the old favourites have had to fight for a place here. Only once we were satisfied that

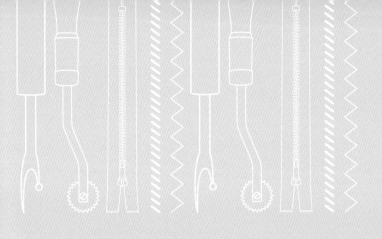

either they were the only video on a particular subject or they really were the best around, did they get page space.

The same rigour was applied to our choice of DIY projects. They had to be inventive, do-able, technically correct and great to look at. And whether they were sew-from-scratch or re-modelled pieces, they had to pass muster with a panel of researchers ranging from twentysomethings to fiftysomethings for broad appeal and edgy detailing. And if some designers of the DIY projects appear more than once, that's because, like the technique videos, they really are the best on YouTube right now!

How to View the Clips

Each entry is accompanied by a QR code, which you can scan with your digital device using apps such as Quick Scan, QR Reader or ScanLife. Alternatively there is a short URL address which you can type into your browser. Unfortunately the adverts preceding some of the clips are unavoidable but it's usually possible to skip them after a few seconds.

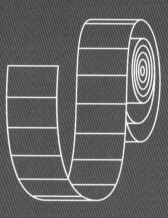

TOOLS

of the Trade

Get to Know Your Sewing Machine

Bookwormshay takes you
on a tour of a basic machine

With fewer than 30 views at the time of writing, this
may not be the most popular video of all time, but it
does a great job of showing you around a standard
home sewing machine. Using a pinboard device to
focus on each part of the machine in turn, it's
entertaining to watch, while giving accurate
technical information. Each part is labelled and easy
to see as Shaylia Johnson explains in layman's terms
how it works and demonstrates exactly what it does.

How to Thread a Sewing Machine

Designer, maker and author
Lisa Comfort gets you set up

Shot in her light, bright London sewing café, Lisa takes you step by step through the process of threading up sewing machines. As most are threaded in pretty much the same way (and have been since the original Singer days), you'll be able to follow her video even if your machine is made by a different manufacturer. But just to make sure, Lisa explains that some bobbins have cases and are put into the machine differently.

http://youtu.be/05kbw8ylfdA

Overlocker Know-How

Mastering an overlocker (serger)

Sarah guides you through the parts of an overlocker, then demonstrates how to thread it up. Known as an overlocker in Britain and a serger in the US, this machine uses three or four needles to create a fabulous professional finish to seams, overwhipping and trimming them in a single action. It's also great for sewing stretch fabric. The overlocker doesn't replace the sewing machine, but if you become a keen stitcher, you may well decide to invest in one. Threading up the four needles is notoriously tricky, and it might all seem a little challenging … but Sarah offers tips and tricks to get you through.

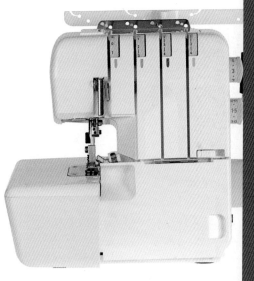

11 You Tutorial

Choosing Sewing Machine Needles

Dee discusses the different machine needles available

Comprehensive, no-nonsense information is what puts this video ahead of anything else on choosing sewing machine needles. Dee explains why each needle has two different size numbers, then runs through the different types: universal (for most fabrics), ballpoint (for jersey), leather, metallic, double, triple and wing needles. What she doesn't do is explain that you need to match the size of the needle to the weight of the fabric. If in doubt, try a couple of sizes on sample fabric and choose the one that creates the most even stitches without any puckering.

http://youtu.be/3a033FwDuJA

Presser Foot Perfection

Everything you need to know about choosing and using presser feet

This clear, instructional video guides you through the uses of the most popular presser feet and how to work with them. Running for nearly 20 minutes, this is hardly a quick look, but it is a useful, comprehensive overview and an informative resource if you want to go out and buy a specialist foot. Made by the Singer Sewing Company, the video has authority, but if you have another make of machine, be aware that there may be differences.

The Beginner's Toolkit

Get off the starting block
with this basic kit

Cutesy BioNerd has just started sewing classes and is all excited about her basic kit-in-a-box, which she rattles through before rushing off to "school". This was clearly the start of something big for her: four years later, she's graduated on to hugely inspirational tutorials with more than half a million subscribers. For this kit, she covers all the pertinent points about needing several different cutting tools, choosing proper shears (long-bladed, angled, heavy) and the basic marking and measuring tools. Fun to watch, the only piece of advice that most sewers would disagree with is using an "exactor knife", or scalpel, instead of a stitch ripper for fear of damaging the fabric. This is the basic kit for starters on a budget.

http://youtu.be/iFx3bZ4StS4

An Expert's Choice of Cutting and Measuring Tools

Insider knowledge from the Thrifty Stitcher

Claire Louise shares the secrets of her favourite sewing tools, including why she has two measuring tapes and why she wouldn't be without her flexible ruler. Shot in her London studio, where she runs sewing classes, Claire Louise also tells us how to prioritize our spending (surprisingly, it's the little scissors she chooses, not the big, for example). Delivering with a hint of a giggle, she's great to watch, and, as the technical advisor to the popular TV show *The Great British Sewing Bee*, she couldn't be more respected for the quality of her knowledge.

Pressing Tools

Beyond the iron and
board: a tailor's view

A pattern designer and instructor with a passion for impeccable tailoring, Angela Wolf shares professional pressing techniques. Steaming her way through irons, boards, tailors' hams and clappers, she demonstrates the techniques tailors have used for centuries to press and shape. Pressing-as-you-go is an essential part of sewing. Use it to open the seams and flatten and shape the part-made garment, so that it will be easier to fit the pieces together perfectly at the next stage of construction. Effortlessly enthusiastic, Angela brings what is usually a tediously dull subject to life. Anyone who wants to make clothes that look handmade rather than home-made should take note!

http://youtu.be/5iTBW0fkNWE

Hand-Sewing Needles

Choosing the right roles
for the smallest players

An exciting delivery on choosing hand-sewing needles was always going to be a challenge. For this video, the focus is appropriately close in on the needles themselves, which are hardly visually exciting. This tutorial would have been very dull indeed if it weren't for the fascinating content, delivered in Professor Pincushion's inimitable, clearly comprehensive fashion. As well as discovering the difference between sharps, betweens, milliners, beading, darning needles and more, we learn about needle threaders and traditional tomato pincushions with their strawberry emery sharpeners.

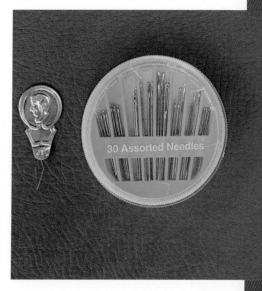

30 Assorted Needles

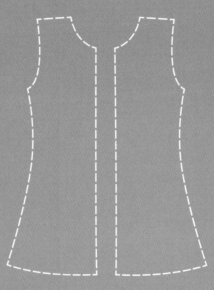

CHOOSING
and Using Patterns

Taking Your Measurements, Choosing Your Size

When size comes down to numbers

Using a mannequin and tape, Professor Pincushion shows us exactly where we need to take measurements and how to take them accurately. Then she draws her beautifully manicured nails down the columns of numbers on the back of the pattern, and explains how to choose the right size for our vital statistics and figure silhouette. She reminds us (both at the beginning and near the end of the video) that we need a considerably larger pattern size for sewing than the one we would choose for ready-to-wear. This reassures us that it is NOT a diet we need, but properly fitting clothes.

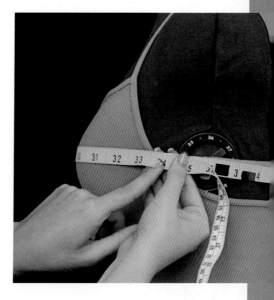

Working Out Fabric Quantities

Professor Pincushion on finding
the information you need

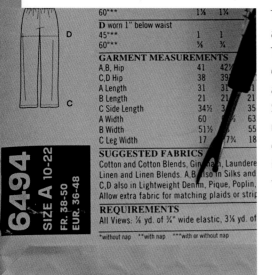

	60"***		1¼	1¼
	D worn 1" below waist			
	45"***		1	1
	60"***		¾	¾

GARMENT MEASUREMENTS

A,B, Hip	41	42½	
C,D Hip	38	39½	
A Length	31	31	
B Length	21	21	21
C Side Length	34½	3	35
A Width	60		63
B Width	51½		55
C Leg Width	17	7¾	18

SUGGESTED FABRICS
Cotton and Cotton Blends, Gingham, Laundere
Linen and Linen Blends. A,B also in Silks and
C,D also in Lightweight Denim, Pique, Poplin,
Allow extra fabric for matching plaids or strip

REQUIREMENTS
All Views: ⅞ yd. of ¾" wide elastic, 3⅛ yd. of

*without nap   **with nap   ***with or without nap

6494

SIZE A 10-22

FR. 38-50
EUR. 36-48

The inimitable Professor Pincushion takes us on another tour of the back of the pattern envelope. This time, it's to help us work out exactly what kind of fabric we need, what haberdashery (notions), and exactly how much of each for our project. She reminds us that, although the numbers given may look intimidating, two-thirds of them can be eliminated at first glance. With Professor Pincushion, it is detail that counts: everything is explained down to the last asterisk.

http://youtu.be/zSa10SeNecg

Understanding Pattern Markings

Colleen G Lea on deciphering sewing symbols

It can be the hieroglyphics of sewing symbols that put people off using commercial patterns, despite the fact that the meanings of the symbols are listed on the instruction leaflet in the pattern envelope. It's very reassuring to take a trip around the pattern pieces with Colleen and see exactly where the different symbols are used, why they are there, what they mean and how they can help us. For more detail, Colleen suggests you follow the link to her blog, where there are historical posts on different symbols.

Adjusting the Pattern for Bigger Hips

Smoothing over the curves
the professional way

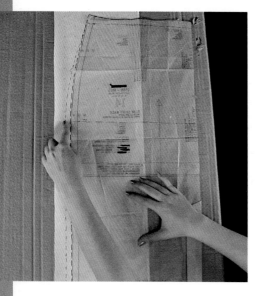

If your waist measurement matches the one given for your chosen pattern size but your hips are a little more generous, you'll need to alter the pattern to fit. Professor Pincushion divulges the tricks of the trade, using the pivot method to create a smooth line that should flatteringly skim your figure without gaping or puckers. As always, she delivers with clarity and simplicity, starting with the maths and finishing with a pattern piece that should sew up into a perfect fit.

http://youtu.be/-z62cxguUOw

Adjusting the Pattern for Smaller Hips

Slimming the hips with Professor Pincushion

Addressing anyone with slimmer hips or a more boyish figure, Professor Pincushion explains the same pivot method she used to adjust the pattern for a more generous hip measurement, only the other way around. Much of the information, such as consulting size charts and working out the maths, is repeated on both videos, so there's no need to refer back and forth from one to another. There's nothing fancy in the presentation; for pattern-altering techniques, it is the information that counts. Shot simply with an overhead camera, both videos are clear, easy to see and easy to understand. As always, Professor Pincushion gets the priorities right.

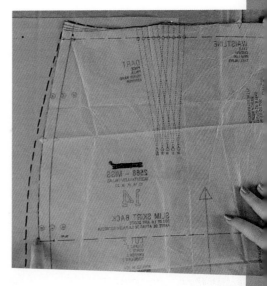

Adjusting the Pattern for a Larger Waist

Comfort and ease
for the waistline

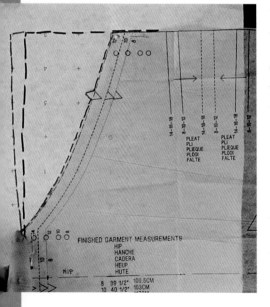

Running to over 20 minutes, this is nevertheless one of Professor Pincushion's most useful tutorials. Using the pivot-and-slide method, she demonstrates the technique for adjusting all the pattern pieces you may need to alter to accommodate a more comfortable waist measurement. Starting with the bodice, she shows how to match the skirt pattern pieces, and explains what to do if that skirt or dress has a pocket. She also covers the information you may need to adjust the waistline on a pair of shorts, and finishes off with waistband alterations. By following through on all the pieces, you can be sure they will fit together perfectly once you come to constructing the garment.

http://youtu.be/gJCnvifLSjQ

Adjusting the Pattern for a Smaller Waist

Slimline fitting for
a neat waistline

This is the companion tutorial to Professor Pincushion's demonstration of Adjusting the Pattern for a Larger Waist (see opposite). If you have an hourglass figure, you're very likely to need to reduce the waistline. Sometimes, though, it can be difficult to decide whether you want to increase the hips or reduce the waist to make the pattern fit. Some patterns do give guidance but if yours doesn't, and it's not at all clear which size you should choose, generally the answer is to go for the size that matches your largest measurement (your hips, maybe) and adjust the other measurements. The only exception to this is if you have a larger bust size (see Making a Full Bust Adjustment, page 30).

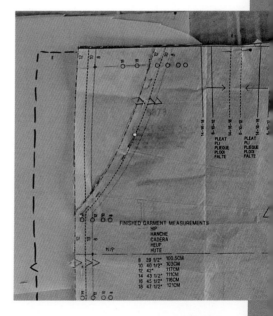

What's the Point of Bust Darts?

Angela Wolf on the why
and where of bust darts

Bust darts are the essential way to make feminine-shaped clothes in non-stretch fabric, but if they're in the wrong place, they look worse than if they weren't there at all. In just over a minute, Angela Wolf responds to a *Threads* magazine reader question and explains why you need darts and where they should be. She also reveals some design tricks both for the big-busted and the svelte. Her last trick is just perfect if you're sewing for slender young teens (or they're sewing for themselves) who would like womanly clothes but don't yet have the curves to fill them.

http://youtu.be/InaJ9GLAGPc

Raising and Lowering the Bust Dart

Colleen G Lea shows how simple it is to raise or lower bust darts

Armed with Angela Wolf's advice on where dart points should lie (see What's the Point of Bust Darts?, opposite), you're ready to adjust the dart positions if you need to. In two videos, Colleen shows how to measure and redraw the darts to suit your figure. She simply raises or lowers the darts, but you can use the same principle if you want to adjust the point either further towards the centre or outwards towards the seam. The key is to draw the dart legs so they finish in the same place as the originals. While professional pattern cutters can move the darts to a different position altogether, home sewers would do well to avoid this … unless you've taken a pattern-cutting course. If you want to raise your bust dart:

http://youtu.be/h1zSgLFH4mY

If you want to lower your bust dart:

http://youtu.be/5oSELKBxUeE

Adjusting the Pattern for a Smaller Bustline

Reducing fullness the Professor Pincushion way

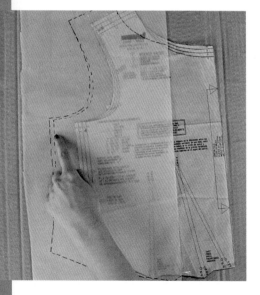

Here's another of Professor Pincushion's invaluable tutorials on pattern adjustments, this time showing how to adjust for a smaller bustline. In her demonstration, the pattern has darts running from the waistline up to the bust point, so in this case, by adjusting the sides, the darts remain untouched. However, in the readers' comments section, she says that if you have side darts, while you may not need to move them, she recommends making a muslin from cheap fabric to check the fit before sewing the final garment. No apologies for recommending Professor Pincushion for all these pattern adjustments: hers really are the best we could find.

http://youtu.be/PLLtBcze4r8

Adjusting the Pattern for a Larger Bustline

Perfecting the
pivot method

If your bust size is any larger than a B cup, you'll probably need to adjust the pattern before you lay it out. Professor Pincushion tells us how to do this using the pivot method, explaining how to take your measurements and how to work out the maths. She then takes us step by step through the pivot method, which allows for extra fabric in the side seams and adjusts the armhole. This is the best method to use if you are a C or D cup. If you have a larger cup size than that, you'll need to make a different kind of adjustment using the pivot-and-slide method. Find out how to do this in the next video (see Making a Full Bust Adjustment, page 30).

Making a Full Bust Adjustment

Iconic Patterns on
curvy girl adjustments

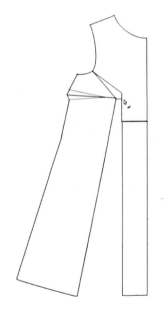

Large-busted women often have to buy clothes that are too large for their frame, which is why many start sewing in the first place! When making your own, you need to choose the pattern size that fits the rest of your body and adjust the bustline using what pattern cutters call the Full Bust Adjustment (FBA). Your high bust measurement will tell you what size pattern to choose for a garment that fits through the chest and shoulders. The difference between this measurement and your full bust measurement will be the figure you need to work out the maths. In less than two minutes, Iconic Patterns shows you how to adjust the pattern using simple computer drawings of the pivot-and-slide method. So simple and so clear!

http://youtu.be/--lin7X3Vxc

Adjusting the Length of Bodice Pattern Pieces

Professor Pincushion on adjusting a bodice pattern

Not many of us have bodies that fit the pattern standard, so Professor Pincushion shows how to work out whether you have a longer-than-average torso or a shorter one. Always adjust the length of a pattern before you attempt the width. For classic petite figures, she points out how commercial patterns have a built-in shortcut for you to follow. For the rest of us, Professor Pincushion demonstrates both how to lengthen a bodice pattern to fit the professional way and how to shorten it. It's a simple "eureka" moment, even for seasoned sewers.

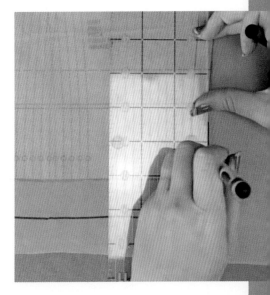

http://youtu.be/YynfVXhPNWA

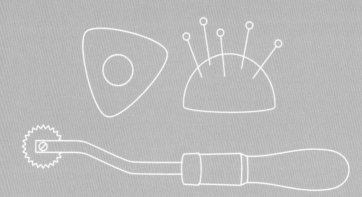

LAYING OUT

and Transferring the Markings

Selvedges, Grain and the Right Side of the Fabric

Emily Tao throws light on all-important fabric details

In this simply but delightfully presented video, Emily Tao explains exactly what the terms "selvedge" and "grain" mean … the all-important information you need to know before you lay out your fabric. Once you understand the terms, and if your fabric is full width with both selvedges, it's easy to work out the grain lines and the right side of most fabrics. But all is not always clear, especially if you have a fabric scrap with no selvedges, so Emily also offers clever clues to help even seasoned sewers discover which is the straight grain and which is the right side of any fabric.

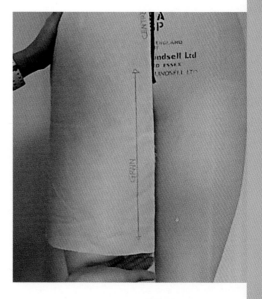

http://youtu.be/Ln0nltbSsao

Cutting Out the Pattern Pieces

Selecting and preparing
the tissue pattern pieces

It might seem obvious that before you can cut out the pattern, you need to select and prepare the pattern pieces, which might be why there is a dearth of YouTube videos on this subject. But get it wrong and you could be in all kinds of trouble, which would certainly lead to a waste of time and possibly a waste of fabric. No apologies for coming back to Professor Pincushion. In 11 minutes, she covers everything you need to know and adds in a few personal tips.

http://youtu.be/F025v6FvGi4

Tissue-Fitting a Pattern

Gertie demonstrates how to fit a pattern on your body

There are many ways to fit a pattern, and all the previous videos deal with adjusting the flat pattern pieces. If you're sewing a close-fitting garment, however, you may prefer to fit the pattern to your body. Gertie's cool vintage style means she's had plenty of fitting experience, and she communicates clearly. Talking us through in plenty of detail, she leaves little room for doubt as she fits the pattern on her own body. The downside (or maybe not) is the long running time of the tutorial: Gertie presents the technique over three videos, running to a total of nearly 25 minutes.

Part 1
http://youtu.be/3TDC0WUyYDc

Part 2
http://youtu.be/Jlng1NIFdak

Part 3
http://youtu.be/D5GWFlkfFlA

How to Lay Out Pattern Pieces

Perfect preparation: the essential first steps to great end results

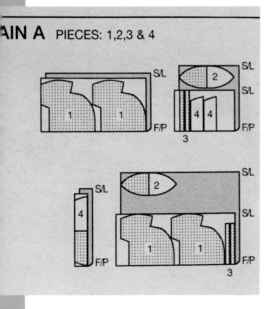

AIN A PIECES: 1,2,3 & 4

In her own inimitable way, Professor Pincushion leaves no stone unturned, from laundering the fabric before you begin (to pre-shrink and remove dressings) to smoothing the pieces as you pin. Obvious as this might all seem, even the videos of some commercial pattern manufacturing companies are not as thorough, possibly because they want to keep their tutorials short. Professor Pincushion is more concerned with giving comprehensive information, and her video stretches to almost 20 minutes. She has hundreds of tutorials under her belt and is refining them all the time, responding to comments left on her YouTube channel. This updated version of laying out the pattern pieces is an excellent example.

http://youtu.be/lNjulZzkTL8

Efficient Pinning

Kat shows how
to pin like a pro

If you're new to dressmaking, you may wonder how seasoned sewers manage to pop in pins so efficiently. Certainly, many people at beginner classes feel a little cack-handed as they tussle with their fabric, which results in less-than-accurate pinning. Using long pins and pretty pink spotted fabric, Kat clearly reveals all, telling us which pins are easiest to use and how to pin while keeping the fabric flat. She then demonstrates where to place and how to space pins, plus the best pivot action to get them in quickly and neatly.

Transferring the Markings

A bird's-eye view of all
the marking methods

If you want a quick overview of all the different ways of transferring pattern markings to fabric, take a look at Cyberseams. In less than two and a half minutes, you will know about all the different tools and materials, plus how to use them. Easy to watch and set to music, which gives the video an almost dance-like quality, there's no voiceover, just labels to name each method. Clearly set in a working sewing studio it's an efficient, refreshing alternative to classic tutorials.

http://youtu.be/3pSXcGle3bo

Notches and Tack Marking

Two tailor-favourite
marking methods

Simple, stylish, clear and informative, this video by
Coats shows two ways to transfer markings, without
special equipment. Tailors and dressmakers have
used notches and tacks for centuries to transfer
markings. Using just a pair of scissors and a needle
and thread, they're still two of the most accurate
and efficient ways to do so, leaving no residue and
not damaging the fabric. It's all demonstrated in less
than five minutes in a fresh, modern presentation
that's easy on the eye and easy to follow.

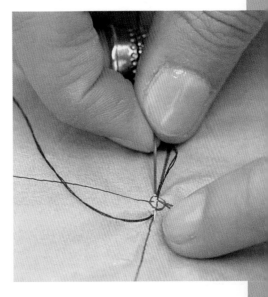

Transferring Markings with Pins

The pin method of marking patterns

If you were intrigued by pin marking in Cyberseams' video (see Transferring the Markings, page 38) and want to give it a go, take a look at this tutorial in which Colleen G Lea demonstrates the technique clearly. Whatever method you use, it's important to transfer the marks accurately through every layer of fabric, otherwise the pieces won't match up properly and you won't get a professional finish. Many people make the marks through all layers using the pins, which is easier to do accurately than with pens and less time-consuming than repositioning the paper to mark each layer separately. They then mark those positions with fabric marking pens, so the pieces are easier to handle during the construction process.

http://youtu.be/UKoB1wu7QzU

STITCHERY

Know-How

Hand Sewing: How to Tie the Knot

Threading the needle,
tying the knot

Even the most sewing-machine-savvy among us couldn't get away with working an entire project without picking up a hand needle and thread. You'll need to tack (baste), slipstitch, hem and sew on fastenings, but before you do any of that, you'll need to know how to thread and knot the needle. In under 40 seconds, Zede Donohue, with her leopard-print nail polish, demonstrates the easiest way to knot the end of sewing threads. While experienced sewers just roll the thread between their fingers and thumb for a perfect knot, beginners can find the technique difficult to grasp. This is the industry standard how-to for beginners.

http://youtu.be/HdcDm21I8VE

A Sampler of Hand Stitches

One-stop hand-stitch guide
with Pandemic Apparel

Starting with making a tailor's knot between the
thumb and fingers, this sampler of hand stitches
quickly gives an overview of the most useful stitches
and what they're used for, including back stitch, pick
stitch, various tacking (basting) stitches and a
selection of hem stitches. Worked with black thread
on cream calico, this video is fuss-free, easy to follow
and a great overview from a tailoring professional.

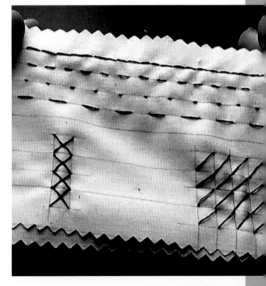

Hand Tacking (Basting)

The temporary solution to smart sewing

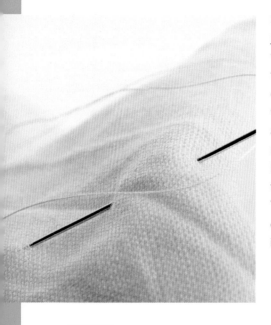

Sometimes, pinning pieces together before sewing just isn't quite good enough. Instead, you might want to stitch them together temporarily using tacking (basting) stitches. Beginners often want to do this for every seam, as then there's no problem with getting pins stuck in the machine foot, and also because tacked, rather than pinned, pieces are more manoeuvrable. But even experienced sewers like to tack when they are working with tricky fabrics such as silks or satins that can slip as you sew. You'll also want to tack pieces together at the more complicated stages of construction, such as setting in sleeves or inserting zips. Here's how to do it.

http://youtu.be/YsRer8fI8Eo

Machine Tacking (Basting)

Jennifer Wiese's
useful guide

There are times when you'll want to stitch pieces together temporarily by machine. This could be in exactly the same situations you may have used hand tacking (basting). Machine tacking is most useful, however, for temporarily stitching long seams, perhaps when you'd like to make final adjustments to a garment at a later date, such as a wedding dress (brides often lose weight as they approach the big day). You can whip through the long seams for fittings, leaving the final stitching to nearer the time. Jennifer Wiese shows us how to machine tack, and, more importantly, how to remove the stitches easily.

Even Slipstitch

Closing the gap the secret way

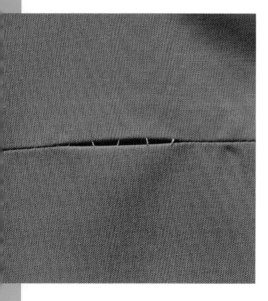

There are two kinds of slipstitch: even and uneven. Even slipstitch is usually used to close a gap or to join two pieces of folded fabric. It is really useful for home furnishings, such as cushion making, but it is also used in dressmaking – for finishing off the ends of bias tape. Uneven slipstitch is commonly used to blind stitch a hem, as shown in the Coats' video (see Sewing a Double-Fold Hem Using Slipstitch, page 98). There are plenty of videos showing uneven slipstitch, but this is one of the few that illustrates clearly how to use it to join two folded edges.

http://youtu.be/QBoYFSxTVc4

Catchstitch

Hands-on tailoring
trick with Gertie

This really useful tailoring stitch can be used to work
between layers in fabrics, such as when constructing
coats and jackets with facings and interfacings.
Although it was covered in Pandemic Apparel's video
(A Sampler of Hand Stitches, page 43), catchstitch
can be difficult to imagine in action, but Gertie
shows us how on her jacket, which looks fabulous,
even on the inside. Chatting us through the process,
she comes up with useful tips as she goes. Stitches
like this really need to be shown, not told, so it's a
million times easier to understand on video than it
ever could be in a book.

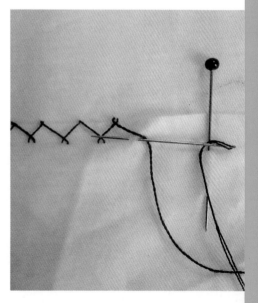

How to Use a Stitch Ripper

Ripping yarns with
Professor Pincushion

Whether you're cooking, sewing, knitting, woodworking or making anything at all, the key to success is being able to put any wrongs right. If you've never used a stitch ripper, this is worth a glance. Most sewing machines come supplied with a stitch ripper, but if yours doesn't, don't be tempted to use any other kind of knife, or even scissors – you'll be in danger of cutting into the fabric. Just get a ripper!

http://youtu.be/bu0il4GxUa8

Tension

Tension problems fixed
by Sewing Republic

A dynamic trip through diagnosing tension problems and getting them fixed, this video tutorial is one of the most thorough on the subject. Packed with information, in two and a half minutes we're served with plenty of easy-to-understand technical information, given practical hints and tips, such as working stitch samples before embarking on any project. We're also shown exactly what to do in every tension scenario. The wrong stitch tension ruins projects and causes time-wasting frustration, so if you don't know how to deal with it, this is a must-see before you start sewing.

Thread Jams

Unblocking those
stitching tangles

ARRGGHHH! Thread jams! It's enough to make a beginner end that sewing love affair before it's begun. Never fear, the glamorous Jennifer Wiese, who looks like she's never had a jam in her life, comes to the rescue. She reassuringly starts off by telling us that thread jams did nearly drive her to giving up, but then she takes us on a step-by-step journey of diagnosis and treatment, so you can get that machine humming again. Most of the tricks come down to getting the threading and tension right, but she throws in extra tips on hunting down and destroying those tangled mats of thread.

http://youtu.be/TT8qvyb39O4

The Basic Machine Stitches

Gypsy Red on machine
stitch solutions

This practical run-through of the most commonly
used machine stitches includes straight stitch,
zig-zag stitch, triple stitch, stretch stitch and machine
overlock stitch. The tutorial has been chosen for its
content, rather than its appearance – the end sample
with its wonderful crop of dangling threads isn't
glorious. But this feels like a real-time presentation
on a stitch sample that isn't trying to be beautiful
in any case.

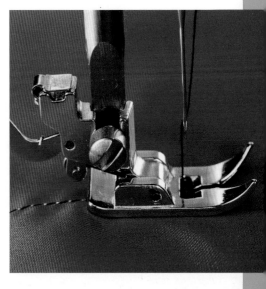

Machine-Stitching Basics

Starter's orders from
Zedes Sewing Studio

Mallory gets right in there to stop you making the classic beginner's mistake. "Do not watch your needle," she warns emphatically (several times). Excellent advice! The natural inclination for beginners is to watch the needle when they should be watching a guide. There are plenty of tips and tricks here on getting your stitches even along straight and curved edges, using "painter's tape" and the edge-stitch foot (great for intermediate sewers). This is one of Zedes Sewing Studio's best videos, combining their chatty style with plenty of invaluable information.

http://youtu.be/t2KremZ6rB8

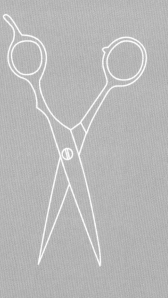

BASIC

Techniques

How to Sew a Single-Fold Clean Finish

Smart seam insider tips
from *Threads* magazine

Joining the seam is only the first step. If you want to stop the edges from fraying or unravelling, you need to finish them off. There are several ways to do this, which are shown in videos reviewed on the following pages. This is the basic one, very neatly done, which you will be able to manage even if all you have is your great-grandmother's ancient Singer sewing machine. This *Threads* video is clean, simple and effective. In 30 seconds, you will have learned how to get the seam straight, flat and neat.

http://youtu.be/pXYMn7woxUY

Neatening Edges with Pinking Shears

Clever clipping
with Colleen

If you're working with a heavy fabric, turning over and stitching the edges to finish will result in unsightly, bulky seams. If there is no zig-zag stitch on your machine, and you don't have an overlocker (serger), the solution is to use pinking shears. Shot live, we watch as Colleen sews and cuts through the whole length of the seam, so it takes more than three minutes to explain. But it's worth watching. With her hallmark clear, easy delivery, adding tips and tricks as she goes, Colleen explains what pinking shears are, how they work and how to use them to best effect.

http://youtu.be/EQq7n1A2QNM

Zig-Zag Seam Finishing

Stitching a neat finish if you don't have an overlocker

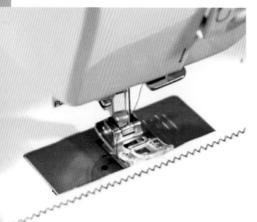

It's the details that make this video stand out from other tutorials on zig-zag finishing. Although the stitches are not very visible at the beginning of the video, the camera soon gets in close, so you can really see what's going on when fashion graduate Aneka Truman stitches down the other side of the seam. As she does, she gets down to the nitty-gritty of the exact stitch length and width you need to set. Shot simply and cleanly in her beautiful studio in the English countryside, this video is a delight to watch.

http://youtu.be/Hi0jN4wlUbA

Finishing the Seams with an Overlocker

Seam finishing the neat, professional way

Easy to watch! Just sit down with Stephanie and she'll explain how an overlocker (serger) works and how to finish seams quickly, easily and professionally. She has a refreshing style: most overlocker tutorials are either scary marketing exercises or rather long, drawn-out and confusing demonstrations by amateur sewers. The tutorial is shot so you can really see what is going on – how the machine sucks in the fabric, then cuts as it sews. In explaining that the overlocker does not replace the sewing machine, Stephanie gets it just right on the finishing.

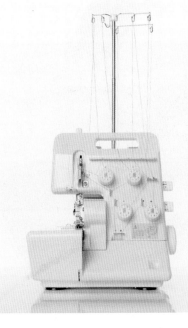

http://youtu.be/ZMKk8Yb1I4k

French Seams

The classic
enclosed seam

Aneka not only makes her video tutorials a delight to watch, but she packs them with plenty of valuable information too. This one gives you everything you need to know about neat, enclosed French seams: why they are used, which fabrics to use them on, exactly how wide a seam you need to take at each stage, precisely how closely the first stage needs to be trimmed and how to press the finished piece. She hasn't yet put up many tutorials, and this one literally popped up while the book was being researched, so we're proud to say that we were one of the first to view!

http://youtu.be/mxuyM5j-rn8

Flat Felled Seams

Perfect classic
jeans seams

The companion to Aneka's French Seams tutorial (see opposite), this is produced just as charmingly and effectively, both in looks and content. Everyone would recognize the flat felled seam as the kind that often runs down the outside of jeans. It is robust and, like the French seam, enclosed. It is the details that count in this video. Aneka keeps her threads trimmed and explains why, and again gives exact trim widths. Her fabric choice has a very obvious right side and wrong side, which makes explaining the flat felled seam so much clearer.

http://youtu.be/ODoLrCTxp5o

Two Great Seam Finishes

Judith Neukam on sewing the two most requested seam finishes

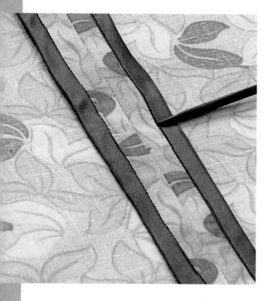

Judith, the Senior Technical Editor of *Threads* magazine, reckons that the two seam finishes her readers ask about the most are the Hong Kong finish and how to use Seams Great, a bias-cut nylon knit binding. With a lifetime of sewing instruction under her belt, Judith has great authority and a clear, calm delivery. Tackling the Seams Great first, she shows us how to make sure we're working with the right side, then how to quickly and neatly stitch it in place. With the Hong Kong finish, she packs her presentation with detail and plenty of tips gathered from years of experience.

http://youtu.be/GTKjjmUvO04

Sewing with Curves

Going round the bend with
Professor Pincushion

Using two small circles of fabric, Professor Pincushion explains how to keep the stitches even as you sew around a bend, how to clip triangles into the seams to make them lie flat, and what they would look like if you didn't (bumpy!). She also shows you how to neatly ease and machine a curved hem using machine gathers. What she doesn't do is show how to deal with convex curves. The answer is: in exactly the same way, except that instead of clipping triangles out of the fabric, you simply snip into the seam allowance with sharp scissors, being careful not to snag the stitches. For more detail, take a look at the next video, Clipping Curves and Trimming Seams (see page 62) by Judith Neukam.

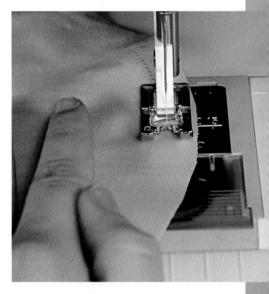

http://youtu.be/0h27ZzDKAB0

Clipping Curves and Trimming Seams

Getting flexibility
into the garment

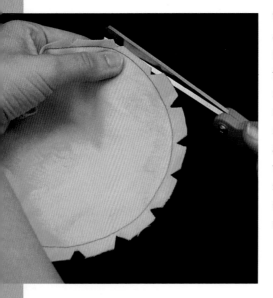

While clipping into curves sounds pretty self-explanatory, Judith shows that there's a lot more to it than meets the eye. By using different-coloured fabrics on different planes (vertical and horizontal), she shows exactly why the seams of some curves need little triangles clipped out of them and others simply need to be snipped to allow more stretch. She also explains where curves should be strengthened with an extra row of stitching and NOT be clipped – such as under arms and the crotch seam of trousers (pants) – or where and why some straight seams need to be clipped to allow for movement.

http://youtu.be/rU2Yu5rwp_s

Sewing into Corners

Pivot-stitching
know-how

Sharp corners demand precise stitching, and there must be absolutely no chance of those stitches slipping or shifting. The solution, which Colleen explains here, is to use the needle-down pivot method, so the fabric can't slip as you swivel it around to sew the next side. It's a simple but useful technique for any corner in dressmaking, such as on collars, cuffs and square necklines, and one you'll use even more frequently if you sew soft furnishings, such as cushion covers and curtains.

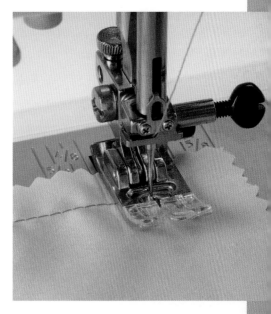

Sharpest Collar Points

The sharpest points
for sharp dressers

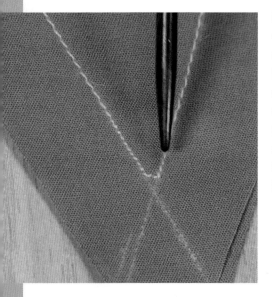

In sewing, everyone has their own tried and trusted ways of perfecting techniques, but Judith Neukam demonstrates that pivoting around a single point isn't always the best way to get the sharpest point, especially if you're sewing an acute-angled collar. By strategically altering the stitch length and making two pivots close together, counter-intuitively, you can stitch a smarter point… but only if you clip away the excess fabric, also explained by Judith with her hallmark clarity.

http://youtu.be/gswGAtQm_yA

The Neatest Way to Mitre Corners

Make neat corner
folds with Colleen

Colleen demonstrates how to mitre a corner, which she explains comes in useful when making details like patch pockets. It's a technique you'll use even more if you want to sew home furnishings, such as curtains, because you will need to mitre the corners at the hemline. Basically, mitring is a very flat, neat, enclosed way to make a corner, and the secret is in the folding. Colleen shows you exactly where to make each fold, and then how to refold the fabric right-sides-together and stitch, so that you get a perfect mitred corner every time.

How to Gather by Hand

Why it's sometimes easier
to gather by hand

As Lex points out in this video, hand gathering stitches don't have to be perfect, or even pretty, as they'll be hidden in the seams of the finished article. And sometimes it's better to gather by hand, especially if you have a heavier fabric. Some people also prefer to hand gather short lengths, such as sleeve heads, because it can be almost as quick to do as on the machine by the time you've fiddled around adjusting the tension and lined everything up. In less than a minute and a half, Lex's dry, witty delivery explains exactly how it's done.

http://youtu.be/o256Ppwf55Q

Machine Gathering: Three Foolproof Ways

Judith Neukam on why and
how to gather fabric by machine

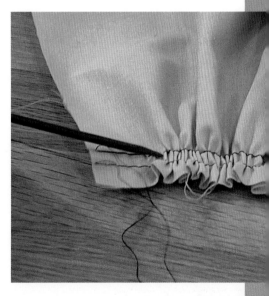

Judith's clear, simple delivery often belies hidden gems, and she springs several surprises in this tutorial on machine gathering. As well as running through all the occasions when you're likely to want to gather, and showing us how to avoid the perennial machine gathering problem of breaking threads, she demonstrates how to pin to a straight edge and still be able to adjust the gathers. And that's just on the first method! She then dishes up two neat alternative techniques: zig-zagging over a heavy thread and gathering using translucent elastic. Judith is a treasure valued by a much younger generation – one comment on this video tutorial said it all: "Wow! How fricking informative!"

Stitching Darts

Professional darts
from start to finish

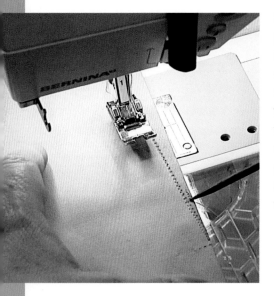

Stitching the darts is the first step in constructing a garment – and for them to look good, they must be stitched and pressed with precision. With a lifetime's experience, Judith Neukam is a reassuring tutor, sharing her tips and techniques for a professional finish. With good, clear, close-up shots, it is very easy to see exactly what is going on at each step and well worth practising first before you get going on your garment. Judith might make it look easy, but there's a knack to getting those stitches so neat and placed with such precision.

http://youtu.be/XW2w9d2WdUw

Sewing Facings

 The what, why and
where of facings

Starting at the very beginning, Judith Neukam introduces this video by explaining what a facing is and where it's used. We learn about interfacings and how to choose and apply them, then she goes ahead and shows clearly how to sew them on and clip the seams. For that ultimate professional finish, Judith explains how and why to under-stitch, and finishes off with pressing. In less than five minutes, you will have learned all the principles about facings that you need to know. Elegantly produced, the tutorial is both easy on the eye and easy to follow.

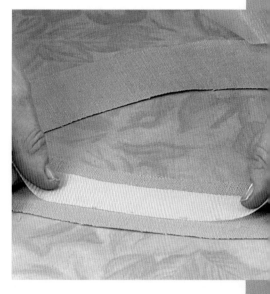

http://youtu.be/YHIigP3_B7k

Every Which Way with Elastic

Seven pretty, spiffy
ways with elastic

This whistle-stop tour whizzes you through all you
wanted to know about using elastic – and more,
from making a casing (which is useful for drawstring
as well as elasticated garments) and stitch-as-you-
go elastic, which is a neat, useful way to finish off
leggings, to working with shirring elastic, making
scrunchies, and variations on those themes. BioNerd
seasons the video with fashion examples of how the
various techniques can be used, and encourages us
to be lateral thinking. After all, she says, that's what
separates a designer from a seamstress!

http://youtu.be/y1ZD88zs6eU

How to Use Shirring Elastic

Straight and even
tips on shirring

Being a photographer as well as a stitcher, Raechel Myers makes videos that are a visual treat! Here, she demonstrates how to use shirring elastic – an essential skill for anyone who wants to make vintage, shirred-back dresses or cute smock-style dresses for little girls. Shirring is a fine, thread-like elastic that can be wound on to the bobbin and used in the sewing machine. Although Raechel adjusts the bobbin tension, this might mess up the tension of your machine, so if you have to, adjust the top tension instead. The most helpful element of the tutorial is how to get those shirring rows straight and even.

Twisty, Twirly Ribbon Using Shirring

A new dimension for trimmings with Lisa Comfort

If you thought that shirring elastic had limited application, take a look at how Lisa Comfort uses it in her sewing café studio. By stitching down the centre of wide ribbons and braids (in this case, a lace one), she turns the trim from flat to frilled, then stitches it on to the neckline of her jumper for a new-look garment in just 20 minutes. Wearing a "one-she-did-earlier" cardigan decorated with two different twisted braids (and one flat one), she brings additional inspiration to the table.

http://youtu.be/50BRupaZFfQ

How to Sew Ricrac

Straight stitching on a wiggly trim

There's a knack to getting any surface trim straight on the fabric, which involves measuring at several points along the hem up to where you'd like the trim to be, then drawing a straight guideline. But when it comes to actual stitching, the wiggly nature of ricrac makes it one of the trickier trims to apply. Colleen G Lea, in her hallmark straightforward delivery, demonstrates exactly how. Shot very close up on the machine foot, it's easy to see exactly where to place the ricrac along the line and exactly how to line up the foot for a professional-looking finish.

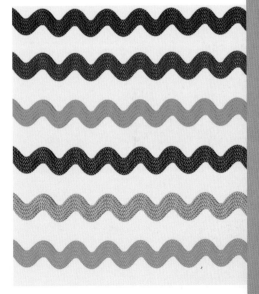

Make Your Own Bias

Cut and fold your
own bias binding

Pattern cutter/fashion designer Ami Lowden starts by showing examples of the many different and wonderful uses for bias binding, from neatly binding seams for a designer finish to using it as a design detail, either in contrast to the main fabric or matching it. The Little Tailoress is clearly highly accomplished when it comes to making bias binding, and has a whole battery of useful tools for making it, including the professional ruler, rotary cutter and a range of bias makers for folding different widths of fabric. The video is packed with hugely useful information on all things bias.

http://youtu.be/Co1tC2NliW8

Making and Applying Bias without Special Tools

A speedy bias
binding overview

If you're going to make loads of bias binding, it's well worth investing in the tools described in the previous video. But measuring, marking and cutting bias without any specialist tools is really not difficult. This video shows you how, using just a steel rule, tailor's chalk, dressmaking scissors and an iron, so there's no need to run out to buy tools before you can get going. It then goes on to demonstrate, step by step, how to stitch on bias for a smart, professional finish. The whole tutorial takes less than two minutes from start to finish!

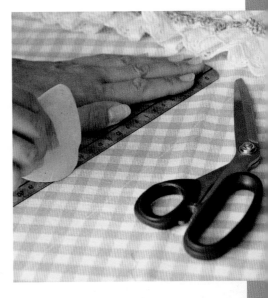

How to Join Bias

Creating extra length
on your bias binding

Although Ami showed beautifully and accurately in Making and Applying Bias without Special Tools (see page 75) how to make bias binding, she didn't show how to join the lengths together. The width of the fabric will limit the length of each strip, and, unless you're binding only a short length, you'll need to join those strips together before you start using them. It does take a bit to get your head around joining them, so that you get a long, straight strip and not a V-shape, with the pieces properly aligned. Follow Colleen's instructions here and you'll get it right first time.

http://youtu.be/obuQzUtdYIQ

Applying Bias Binding

The professional way to a neat finish

Judging by the extremely narrow trim she demonstrates, Ami Lowden (aka The Little Tailoress) is clearly hugely accomplished at applying bias. You might want to start on a slightly wider binding, but follow her method and it's sure to come out with a professional finish. The secret to her success is using the traditional method of stitching twice, combined with her clever pinning method, to make sure the binding is caught in the stitches on both sides down the full length. In demonstrating, she throws in tips about how to use different presser feet and how to extend binding to become spaghetti straps on a top.

Perfect Piping

 The Little Tailoress on
making your own piping

Piping smartens up edges and is currently used less for garments than it is for home furnishings, such as cushion covers. Although Ami Lowden is a pattern cutter/fashion designer, she has nevertheless put up this piping video and demonstrates the technique to fabulous effect on a taupe cushion cover, showing how to make and apply the piping. Her piping is made up of bias binding wrapped around piping cord, and it would also be useful to watch her video on making bias binding (see Make Your Own Bias, page 74). All the steps are very clear, despite being somewhat fiddly. As always, she is thorough and a perfectionist. Her exquisite videos are shot in her beautiful home studio.

http://youtu.be/JonW7JcN1yI

Marking Up for Tucks

Doing the maths for marking
up three kinds of tucks

Commercial patterns featuring tucks show the fold
line for each tuck, but if you want to add tucks to
any garment, you need to know how to mark them
up before sewing. Using an acrylic dressmaker's
ruler, Raechel Myers shows how to mark the folds
and stitch the lines for three kinds of tucks: blind
tucks, spaced tucks and pintucks. She demonstrates
on small squares of fabric and suggests that
beginners do several test squares to begin with.
Once you do get to your project, it can be difficult
to work out how much extra fabric to allow, so the
best plan is to stitch the tucks first, then position
the pattern piece over the ready-tucked fabric for
cutting out the shape.

Stitching Tucks

Smart stitching for
three kinds of tucks

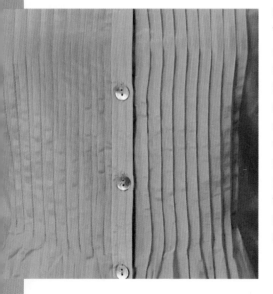

In this, the companion video to Marking Up for Tucks (see page 79), Raechel Myers shows how to stitch and press spaced tucks (where you can see the stitch lines), blind tucks (where the lines are hidden) and pintucks. Demonstrating on small fabric samples, this video, at over 11 minutes long, is pretty much real-time (expect for the pintucks, which she whips off to do mainly off-camera). But somehow it never gets tedious. Tucks are fiddly and, as Raechel points out, they need to be perfectly stitched every time, so it's helpful to see the process close up and right the way through. Prettily produced, informative and easy to watch.

http://youtu.be/lDoNn_xE4m4

How to Set In a Sleeve

Setting in sleeves the professional way

Judith Neukam has a deep understanding of fabric. She knows how it behaves and how to construct garments. She is also a brilliant communicator. She doesn't just explain one dogmatic way to set in a sleeve but explains what works, what doesn't and why, and how different people tackle the problems so that we can choose which method suits us best. Setting in sleeves has confounded many, if not most, sewers over the years, but Judith presents her techniques so effortlessly that she has us all running to our sewing machines, desperate to give it a go. "You see," she says at the end of the video, "sewing in a sleeve isn't at all hard!" That's because she makes it look so easy.

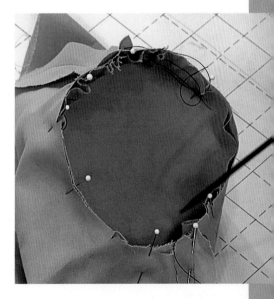

BASIC TECHNIQUES

Setting In a Tailored Sleeve

Machine skills for
tailored sleeves

Tailored sleeves need to be encouraged over the
shoulder without the use of gathering, and Gertie
does this using a strip of bias wool and mohair.
She shows us how to create the curve by stretching
the bias strip and very slightly bunching up the
sleeve head as she runs them together through
the machine. Gertie is clearly a highly accomplished
tailor, and this is not a technique that a beginner
would be advised to try. If you do want to try it,
experiment with fabric scraps before risking
expensive wool material. Even if this isn't something
you'd like to try, it is a fascinating tutorial well
executed by Gertie.

http://youtu.be/Qps2Uy4qSWw

FASTENINGS

and Zips

Stitching Lapped Zips

Step-by-step smart
skirt fastening

Close up, calm and set to reassuringly soothing guitar music, this must be one of the best videos on stitching zips, clearly showing us how to perfectly put in these notoriously tricky customers. This shows the lapped method, with the zip designed to go into skirts or trousers with a single shield folding backwards, covering the teeth. There are some great tips such as how to get past the pull neatly, and using masking tape as a guide to get that final stitching line effortlessly straight.

http://youtu.be/P6nY9av8O3g

Invisible Zips

The stitch-perfect way to insert an invisible zip

The spotty fabric chosen for this video demonstrates just how invisible these zips can be, and the huge satisfaction of stitching them in perfectly. With the spots impeccably lined up and the zip hidden out of sight behind the seam, the only clue that it's there is the pull at the top. Coats has, again, produced a faultless video: stitch-perfect with every step crystal clear. With just over 200 views, there are a whole load of sewers missing out! Coats are thread and yarn manufacturers, so most of their video tutorials focus on tiny embroidery stitches, which makes them well practised in the super-clear, super-close-up videos.

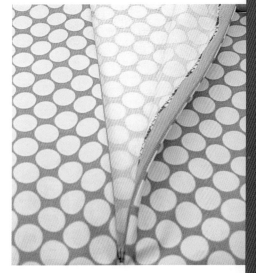

Inserting a Regular Zip

Getting centred on
a regular zip

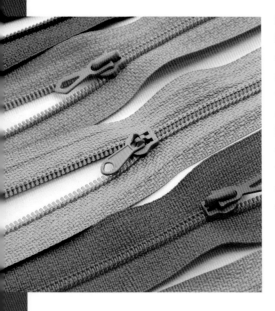

If you prefer a friendly tutorial style, then sitting next to Lisa Comfort in her delightful Sew Over It sewing café in London is a great way to learn how to put in a regular (as opposed to an invisible) zip. She uses the centred method, which was the traditional choice for the back of dresses before the invention of invisible zips and adds authentic appeal to vintage clothes. Lisa is clear in her delivery of every step and throws in tips such as putting the pins in pointing down one side of the zip and up the other, so they're easy to remove as you go.

http://youtu.be/IFMZGMJCmUs

Applying an Exposed Zip

Exposed zips the clean-finish way

Sewing teacher, author and blogger Gretchen Hirst, aka Gertie, combines edgy fashion with perfect sewing, taking us step by step through applying an exposed zip. She points out, continually, that it's all a bit counterintuitive because the raw edges are turned to the right side. This is very reassuring, and by the end of the video, you can see the result is a very neat, clean finish on the inside and funky exposed zip detail on the outside. Gertie has great professional, hands-on tailoring know-how, which comes to life when combined with her own vintage rockabilly style.

Fly Zips

Sorting out the flaps
when sewing in the flies

Let's face it, fly zips can do your head in! They flummoxed the contestants in the TV show *The Great British Sewing Bee*, and most managed to muddle the layers and confuse the construction. So who better to show you how to do it correctly than Claire Louise Hardie, the technical advisor on the show? She holds our hands throughout the whole process, choosing a contrast fabric for the zip shield for clarity. Here's where video tutorials are so brilliant – they can be paused until you're absolutely sure you're ready for the next stage of the challenge!

http://youtu.be/8N-94kEZtP0

Separating Zips

Clear steps for
separating zips

Stitched into the front of jackets and cardigans, separating zips are the focal point of the garment, so absolute perfection is the challenging aim. Coats shows you how. Professionally shot with excellent lighting and a sharp focus so close that you can see every single thread in the fabric weave, the clarity makes this video extremely easy to follow. This take-your-time tutorial encourages an unhurried approach, showing us every time we come to the slider exactly how to slide it away from the stitching line. The combination of easy-on-the-eye blue and grey fabric, plus soothing background music, encourages calm confidence when sewing this admittedly tricksy technique.

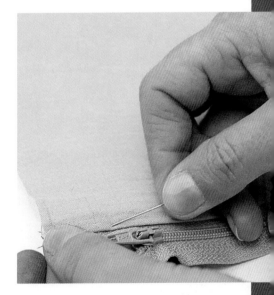

http://youtu.be/Lxvdx7Pb-20

Sewing on a Button by Hand

Clever tricks with matchsticks
when sewing buttons

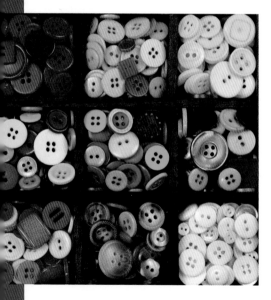

If you don't know how to sew on a button, you're
not alone! In the days when primary school children
were taught to sew, it was a mainstay project. But
not any more, which leaves loads of people at a loss
as to how it's done. This video takes you through
step by step, from measuring to finishing off, and
includes an easy tip for creating a shank using a
matchstick. The shank provides a stalk so there's
room for the fabric to lie behind the button for
(especially) heavier fabrics when they're done up.
Quadrille produces beautiful, snappy, clear video
tutorials, and this is no exception.

http://youtu.be/7-1JuHfuK9Q

Sewing on a Button by Machine

Failsafe way to
machine-stitch buttons

Crisply and clearly, Coats shows exactly how to sew
on a button using a sewing machine, starting with
how to set the machine and ending with the secure
hand finish. No detail is missed, including choosing
the correct presser foot and how to check and
double-check the button size setting, to ensure the
needle doesn't accidentally hit and damage the
button. Simple, easy delivery is not muddled with
incidental chitchat, and the choices of fabric and
thread colours not only make it a visual treat, but
also easy to see and understand what is going on.

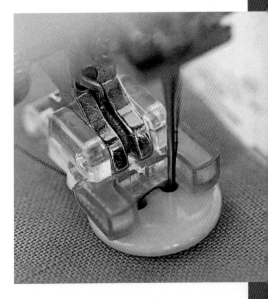

http://youtu.be/q416QdEElts

How to Cover a Button

Tilly's fabric
button tutorial

It's not difficult to cover your own buttons with fabric, using a special kit available from haberdashery (notions) departments. Make them to match your garments, or choose a contrasting fabric to make a design statement. Tilly loves to use vintage fabrics, and since you need only a small amount, even scraps cut from upcycled retro dresses can go a long way. Tilly's put together a simple tutorial of deckle-edged still images with relevant captions. Give yourself a minute and you'll be so won over by her pretty video, you'll be rushing out to get that kit and get covering.

http://youtu.be/tbjPh0G4H0A

How to Machine a Buttonhole

Sew-easy
buttonhole stitching

Just the idea that the buttonholes could make or break the look of your garment was enough to put off previous generations from making something with stitched buttonholes. It's no problem now, as modern sewing machines have turned stitching buttonholes into something of a picnic! Jaime Morrison Curtis, one of the duo of mums that makes up Prudent Baby, demonstrates how easy it is on her ordinary home sewing machine, which has a special gadget to measure the button and stitch the buttonhole all by itself! Always try this out on a piece of folded scrap fabric first, to check the tension and make sure the button fits, then, just like Jaime, away you go. How easy is that?

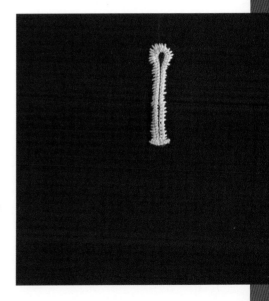

Sewing a Buttonhole with an Older Machine

Stitch-perfect, four-step
buttonholes

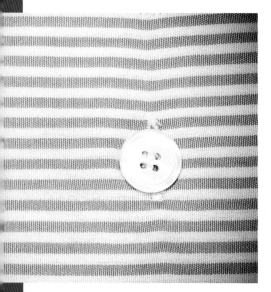

OK, so you might not have a whizzy new electronic machine and you're making do with Mum's (or Granny's) old electric. No worries. As long as it has a swing needle, you can still stitch smart buttonholes by using the zig-zag setting. This video shows how to mark the buttonholes and set them up ready for sewing. Next, using labels, rather than voiceovers, we're told exactly how to set the machine at each stage as we watch the buttonhole being demonstrated. Not quite as foolproof as the automatic method, maybe, but the end result looks pretty professional.

http://youtu.be/gQlnGuUB9wM

Hammer-On Snaps

The no-sew solution
to snaps

Hammer-on snaps are not the only no-sew fasteners
– there are also stock jeans buttons, rivets and
eyelets, many of which come as a pack complete
with the tools you need to apply them. Others need
to be applied with special pliers but, as Raechel
Myers points out, hers have had only one outing
from the pack. Her preferred way is to use a hammer
and her kids' building block. She takes nearly eight
minutes to show us how to do it – all clearly real-
time as she riffles through the snap parts to find
some that aren't bent. But she's easy to watch,
presents delightful videos and somehow, being so
real about the pitfalls as well as the pleasures, she
makes it all just look so much more do-able.

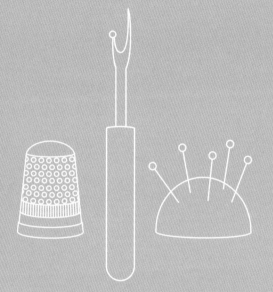

FINISHING

Machine Stitching a Double-Fold Hem

Measuring up for
perfect hem stitching

The key to sewing any hem successfully is to get it straight and get it even, and that can only be done with accurate measuring. Jennifer Wiese demonstrates exactly how to do this using a sewing gauge, then gives hints and tips as to the best way to press and stitch it perfectly into place, all within three minutes. The tutorial is clear and easy to see, and Jennifer has an easy presentational style. There's no extraneous chitchat: she just delivers all you need to know, throwing in a seasoning of useful tips as she goes.

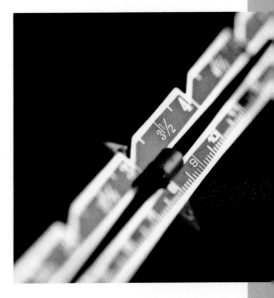

Sewing a Double-Fold Hem Using Slipstitch

Hand-stitching an invisible hem

Slipstitching a hem might not be the most complicated of techniques, but a badly stitched hem can ruin a garment, so you really need to see exactly how it is done. And you really can in this video! Shot super-close-up, you can see every tiny detail: how to pick up just one thread and how to slip your needle through the fold of the fabric. At the end of the video, the fabric is turned over and, if you look hard, you can just about see where the stitches come through to the right side. Job done!

http://youtu.be/lu6llHgoPXw

Herringbone Hemming

Hand-stitching a heavy fabric
the professional way

The hems of heavier fabrics such as wool can look bulky, creating a ridge on the right side of the garment. The solution is to zig-zag finish the raw edge, then use a herringbone stitch. In their inimitable style, Coats show exactly how to work herringbone stitch to a professional finish. Their videos really are a treat to watch. Quite apart from clever fabric selection, which makes the technique easy to see and understand, the hand and machine movements are so beautiful, they look like they've been choreographed. You'll find yourself mesmerized watching how to knot the thread, even before the stitching begins!

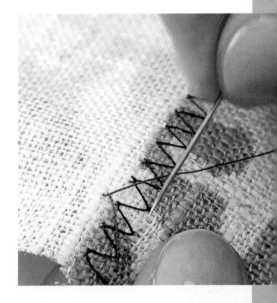

Hemming Stretchy Fabric with a Twin Needle

The professional way to hem stretch fabric

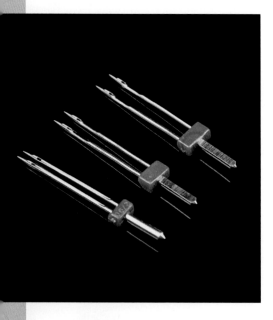

If you want any stretch garment you make, such as T-shirts, to look like you bought them, you'll need to finish off with smart stretchy hemlines that really look the part. The key is to stitch them with twin needles. These make two neat lines of stitching at the front of the work, and a more elastic zig-zag at the back, so that the hem stretches with the rest of the garment. Angela Wolf explains exactly how to get the best results, starting with how to thread the machine and needles, which stitch length to set, and how to machine.

http://youtu.be/kJMTCyV9D50

Using Fishing Line to Make a Curly Hem

Bringing bounce to
sheer hemlines

Wow! This is such a cool idea! Professor Pincushion gives bounce and curl to the hemlines of sheer, cut-on-the-cross skirts by sewing in fishing line as she zig-zags the hem. It's not a Professor Pincushion original idea, but it's a great one for circle skirts with extra bounce for the prom. For such a cute project, it would have been nice to see a finished garment, but Professor Pincushion's videos major on accuracy, rather than image, which is why we chose this over other videos on the subject. The technique is delivered in precise detail (including the use of a toilet roll), so you know it will work and it's not just some wacky idea. And we're liking the professor's prom-pink nails for this one!

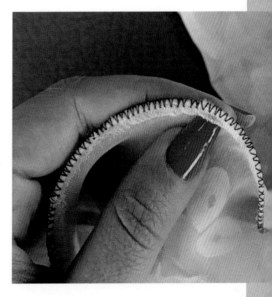

JEANS

Genius

How to Take Up a Pair of Jeans

Tailor dad shows
us the professional way

This is priceless! Hollywoodactress's tailor dad sits cross-legged on the sitting-room floor as he measures up for the alteration, then uses his professional machine to show us how to stitch. It's all good, accurate stuff, and it takes more than 12 minutes. But we don't mind. Hollywoodactress's dad is just a darling, and hollywoodactress isn't an actress at all. He's a London geezer who does a bit of singing in a band and loves his vintage BMW. But he does a great job asking his dad the right questions, so we can get the right answers. Come on, Dad, give us an encore!

http://youtu.be/mBGjiiloDSA

Faking Professional Jeans Stitching

Matching jeans stitching
when you don't have the right thread

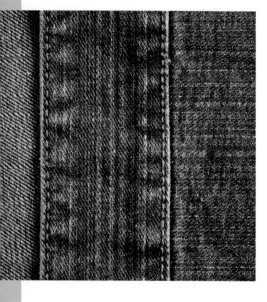

No worries if you want to take up your jeans and match the stitching to the rest of the garment but don't have the right thread. Claire Louise Hardie's clever solution of using dual threads means you can mix and match a couple of colours from your sewing box without having to go out and buy expensive speciality thread. Shot very close, so you can really see what's going on, Claire Louise explains clearly and demonstrates exactly how to thread the machine using a second spool, and then how to produce jeans-style stitching to perfection.

http://youtu.be/828xA7j1p5E

How to Shorten Jeans, Keeping the Original Hem

Three ways to
one classy outcome

This clever trick means there's no unpicking, no amateurish bulky finish, and you can retain the original contrast stitching that matches the rest of the jeans. It works with skinny jeans or any with a straight leg, but you could get into a terrible tangle if you tried it on bootcuts or flares. This might not be Megan and Steph's original idea, but they do it well. The video is clear, classy, and they offer three different ways of finishing off.

Attaching Jeans Buttons

The genuine finish with buttons and rivets

If you want your denims to look believably professional, you'll need to finish them with genuine-article jeans buttons and rivets. What Brian Remlinger doesn't know about jeans buttons and rivets probably isn't worth knowing. Over three video tutorials, he describes all the different designs and where you can get them, and then demonstrates applying them using a hammer. The technique is pretty simple, and for the buttons involves hammering the button part on to a tack pushed through the denim. But Brian chats through all sorts of eventualities, from what might go wrong to how to deal with different weights of denim. With nearly 150,000 views on jeans buttons, Brian is definitely the go-to guy on the subject.

http://youtu.be/qCA35nISC_Y

Transform Your Loose Fits into Skinnies

Failsafe way to upcycle
your jeans

Chris is a cool guy and he knows a thing or two about remodelling jeans. There are plenty of guys out there showing similar transformations, but their technique isn't always correct. On the other hand, Chris, who dresses himself mainly from thrift shops, is clearly a master of the sewing machine. He shows accurately how to measure against favourite jeans, how to sew and, after it's all stitched up and tried on to check the fit, where to cut. His video is beautifully directed, clear, informative and a delight to watch.

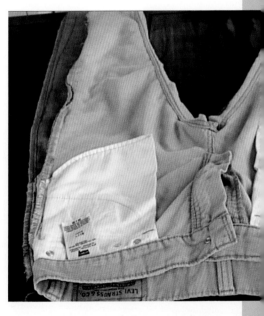

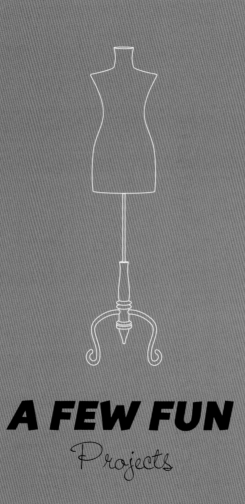

A FEW FUN

Projects

Make Your Own Oversized T-Shirt

How to copy your favourite T-shirt

New sewers often want to copy a favourite garment, which can be easy or difficult, depending on the garment. If you're a beginner, start on something with a loose fit, like Chris's baggy T. There's no dialogue, just labels and hand signals, perfectly executed and perfectly timed, so we know just what we need to do. He describes where and when to sew, but doesn't get into the nitty-gritty of how. Tip: use the stretch stitch on your machine, if it has one. If not, make a line of straight stitch, then zig-zag the seam allowance. Work the hems and necklines with a twin needle (see Hemming Stretchy Fabric with a Twin Needle, page 100). Being Chris, he adds in cool design details like slits in the side seams.

Upcycle an Old Shirt

Remodel your
boyfriend's shirt

Lizzie might not profess to be a trained fashion designer, but she's pretty nifty with the needle. She takes her boyfriend's old checked shirt, nips it in, chops off the sleeves and gives it a new collar with metal chain fastenings. She cuts a pattern from the collar, leaving the original, then makes a new one to slip and stitch over the old one. You could leave it at that but she adds her signature metal detailing and finishes by showing us one she did earlier. It might be similar to the one she demonstrated, but it's not the same. It never would be or could be, which is the whole point of vintage and thrift shop upcycling!

http://youtu.be/jF9C8bml2a4

Little Girl's Shirred Smock Frock

Aussie mum stitches up some treats for her little girl

If the little girl in your life just can't get enough dresses, learn how to smock with shirring elastic (see How to Use Shirring Elastic, page 71), then whizz up as many as she could wish for. Cut them long, cut them short, upcycle some from your own favourite, timeworn clothes, or make some party-style with organza and tulle. This Aussie mum shows and tells how to do it, and also includes measurements. Made from a couple of rectangles of fabric, the frock is as easy as pie. Your greatest reward will be one very happy little girl (or two or more!). Watch this video right to the end and you'll see Aussie Mum's very own little model twisting, turning and swishing the skirt as she models the masterpiece. Ahhh bless!

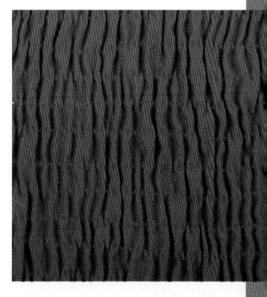

Prettify a Cardie with Lace

New looks for
favourite cardigans

It takes two and a half minutes for Lisa Comfort to demonstrate how to transform an old cardigan into a custom-made designer model, which she says will take just 30 minutes to complete. She chooses a motif that fits the neckline, presumably either using a vintage lace collar or cutting it from a lace fabric length. You'll need a freestyle embroidery foot for your sewing machine and a small amount of iron-on interfacing, and then you can get going.

She demonstrates the knack of using machine embroidery to firmly stitch on the whole body of lace. Lisa has great fresh vintage style and this is a gorgeous way to give your cardigans new life.

http://youtu.be/_jYOxl6ReAQ

Cute Quickie Skirt with Elasticated Waist

A whistle-stop,
quick-sew skirt tutorial

This make-it-in-an-hour skirt is the perfect solution for anyone who has a fab piece of fabric and wants to quickly whizz up something to wear that night. It might look effortlessly easy, but Crafty Amy has clearly had more than a few sewing lessons. She demonstrates the correct way to halve and quarter the waistband, so that it stitches in evenly, and how to stretch the wide black elastic through the machine (which, incidentally, is a key part of her design and does not need to be enclosed). She finishes off with an exposed zip for decorative purposes. If this is a bit swift for you to capture, check out Gertie's more detailed instructions for exposed zips on page 87. Lastly, the hem is finished, and Amy's skirt is hot to trot.

How to Make a Circle Skirt (without a Zip)

Secrets of stitching a
simple-sew skater skirt

Aussie Annika Viktoria shows a clever, tricksy way to make a circle skirt (in this case, a skater skirt, which is a short circle skirt) without having to put in a zip, which can be a challenge. There are zillions of skater skirt tutorials out there but this is easy to follow, clearly works, and she styles it well with a pretty sheer blouse, so she gets our vote! For this great beginner project, Annika Viktoria shows how to make a simple pattern, complete with a formula to work out what size you need to cut out the inner circle, which will be the waistline. Then it's just stitch and go.

http://youtu.be/4ZpFlgD29nl

DIY Maxi Skirt

An awesome
quick-make maxi

If you're confident with a sewing machine, you could create this great maxi skirt in just two hours. From cutting the pattern to the final hem, the video demonstrates the whole process step by step. Watchpoints: when cut on the cross, the skirt hangs beautifully and flatteringly from the hips, but you will need a lot of fabric. Also, while Threadbanger weights the fabric before cutting out, you will want to get out the pins as the bias-cut stretch fabric edges will be super-elastic! A great tip: she sandwiches the seams between tissue paper to control the stretch while stitching. She uses pink tissue, but you'd be better off choosing a shade close to your fabric colour, to avoid any potential colour runs from tiny shreds of tissue caught in the stitches when you wash the garment.

http://youtu.be/KaEvDxFS6XI

Easy Kimono

Transform a scarf into
a must-have kimono

Here's one you can make in 20 minutes, even quicker if you have a sewing machine. Flick the video to 56 seconds and you'll find the key annotated fabric diagram showing where to fold, where to sew and where to cut. Later in the video, Lauren explains how to measure up to work out how much fabric you will need – so rummage remnant boxes and thrift shops for fabulous fabrics and scarves of at least this size that deserve a life in the spotlight. Fine fabrics with a soft drape, such as silk, chiffon or polyester mixes work best. Lauren bravely wears hers over shorts in the Canadian winter, but it can be thrown on over almost anything for a great look, whatever the weather.

http://youtu.be/SmJ8L4VCMjk

Easy Maxi Tent Dress

Step-by-step to a
simple summer staple

Using a favourite tank top as a pattern for the bodice and a few metres (yards) of fabric, Boat People Vintage runs up a simple summer dress. She chooses classy nautical stripes, and raw-cuts the neckline and armholes. If you don't want yours to fray or lose its shape, you may want to make and stitch on facings, or at least overlock, zig-zag or turn in the edges. It's a great idea, beautifully presented, but looking at her cutting diagram, you're going to need a minimum of three metres (yards) of fabric … unless you cut it short, which would be great, too. Cut long or short, this would make a great beach dress.

http://youtu.be/1jO7zt7OAY0

Sassy Silk Top

Classy tops from
vintage scarves

Tutor Tri teaches beginner sewer Lulu how to transform two funky scarves into a fabulous raglan-sleeved top. She starts by showing Lulu how to make the pattern and cut out the fabric. She then gets on with the sewing, taking Lulu through the whole process, step by step, until the top is finished. It's a clever idea because Tri even shows Lulu how to use the sewing machine, answering questions as she goes. So even complete beginners should be able to follow this one and finish up with a fabulous, unique vintage top.

http://youtu.be/POttWNxFx9M

Quickie Cosmetics Bag

Quick and easy, fully lined cosmetics bag

This is such a clever technique! Keryn builds the shell and lining around the zip, then stitches the ends, and finally pinches in triangles at the corners for a fab, easy, boxy shape. It really couldn't be simpler, and it still works if some of the alignment is fractionally skewed because you can sort that out when you sew the side seams. And that's a relief because making box shapes by the traditional method demands precision when it comes to cutting, measuring and seaming together. Once you have the hang of it, you'll be tempted to whizz up bags of all kinds, shapes and sizes.

Easy Off-the-Shoulder Top

A great going-out top
that's easy to sew

Using an everyday tank top to make the basic pattern, this top really does look easy to make. Even beginners should be able to manage, given a little practise with sewing stretchy knit fabric, plus time and patience as they mark, cut and stitch. New sewers would be wise to choose a plain fabric, rather than a stripe as demonstrated, because matching up the pattern can be tricky. Many YouTube DIY sewing projects are college grunge style, left with raw edges, but this finished garment is one that is likely to appeal to a wide age range.

http://youtu.be/g8ti3TlTelU

Peter Pan Collar Dress with a Box-Pleated Skirt

Easy-to-copy design
details in one clever dress

This is one cute dress loads of people would want to make and wear, and April demonstrates how to cut the pattern and sew the dress with a clarity that an intermediate sewer could manage. But where this tutorial is clever is that less confident sewers could take parts of it to use for other projects. For example, it shows how to draft a pattern for – and make – a Peter Pan collar, which is a fashionable design detail that can be used to upcycle dresses and cardigans. It also describes how to box-pleat, a smart, flattering alternative to gathering that's great for making simple skirts without the need for darts. All in just over 12 minutes, little wonder this has had more than 150,000 views and over 5,000 likes!

http://youtu.be/2I2MqGdcvgo

Oh-So-Elegant Silky Jumpsuit

The Q2han twins showcase
a summer classic

Gorgeous, ageless and finished to couture quality, the twins present this exquisite jumpsuit in their inimitable evocative and knowledgeable style. This elegant jumpsuit is certainly not a beginner project, but for keen stitchers, the complete package of how to cut and stitch is encapsulated on the video and delivered within six minutes. They show you how to draw out the pattern, widen the legs using the slash-and-pivot method, then run through the complete construction process. If you have any doubt about the fit, take a tip from professional designers and make it up in cheap muslin first, so you can make adjustments before cutting up your expensive fabrics.

http://youtu.be/DRwQCXNwWJg

Paisley Shorts

Scarves transformed
into shorts

Chris does loads of things with bandana scarves but the best are these shorts. They'd look great in the city, great on the beach and equally as good on girls as boys, depending on the length they're cut and the scarves they're made from. Bandanas are one great thrift solution, easy to buy both from chain stores and online, and adding cool ethnic print to your style. It's a great idea for simple-make shorts using scarves of all kinds. Try upcycling vintage silk scarves for a very different look.

Retro Bikini

From one-piece to
retro-cool bikini

Wow! This really is stunning! Daniela Tabois gets her scissors to an old swimsuit and transforms it into the coolest retro bikini everyone would love to wear. OK, so Daniela has a figure to die for, but these retro cuts really are flattering for all ages. And all you mums and grannies out there thinking high waist is just so 1980s or so 1950s … well, yes, you're right, but as Daniela says, fashion just keeps on coming round. We're loving it, especially as it's great at holding in the tummy and smoothing over the hips.

http://youtu.be/PDJXaNE8JX4

Simple-Sew Chiffon Top

Fabulous top to whizz
up in minutes

Made from just a metre (yard) of pretty printed chiffon, this top is so simple to put together, even a total beginner could manage it. On the other hand, beginners might find the slithery, slippery chiffon hard to handle. No worries, just take your time and, with all that fullness, it wouldn't really matter if the stitch lines aren't knife-edge straight anyway. Newcomers to sewing might be a bit stumped when it comes to the waistline elastic and neckline shirring, but the solution is to check out Every Which Way with Elastic (see page 70).

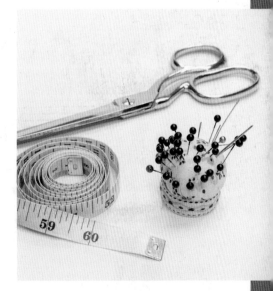

http://youtu.be/qfb9hp_oq_E

Zip-Front Dress

Designer dress from
rectangles of fabric

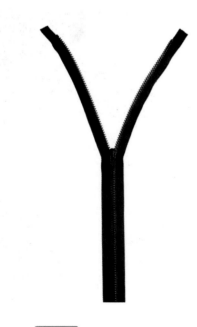

How clever is this! The front zip doubles as smart shoulder straps in a Max Azria-inspired dress that's made using simple rectangles of fabric. With no pattern to cut, no need to trace around a favourite garment, and no darts to sew, you really can't go wrong with the cutting out, and as long as you do your maths right to align the centre-back and centre-front, the stitching up is pretty simple too! Take care with pleating the skirt on to the bodice. Pleating evenly as you go takes a good eye and plenty of practice. If you don't get it right, unpin and begin again. Start stitching only once you're totally satisfied the pleats are evenly spaced.

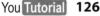

http://youtu.be/XG7vEp831p4

Blazer Reconstruction

Five inspired looks
from one blazer

This is seriously awesome! By chopping off the sleeves, then using tailoring tricks such as pinch-and-pin for fit, and pleating to enhance the silhouette, Threadbanger completely reconstructs an old thrift-shop blazer for not just one, but five, completely different looks. If you like the flexibility of the different styles, she suggests you stitch on snaps, so you can quickly adapt the basic blazer to suit your mood. And it's all delivered in less than three minutes. With neatened edges all round, the finished garment is smart yet cool with more than a touch of Vivienne Westwood-inspired styling.

The Author

Tessa Evelegh is a magazine and newspaper journalist in the UK. She is the author of over 30 books which include *Sewing Made Simple* and the bestselling *The Great British Sewing Bee*, launched with the BBC2 series.

Picture Credits